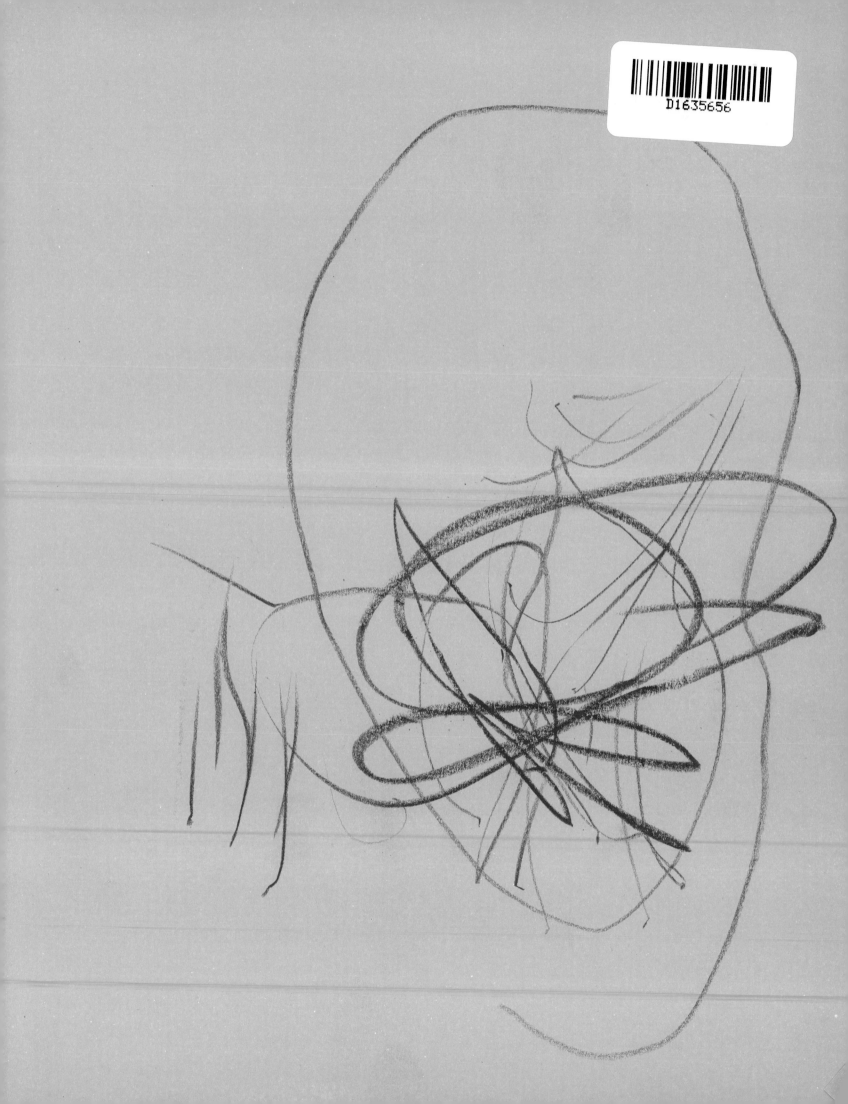

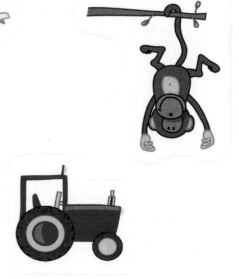

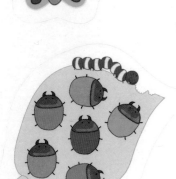

ABC

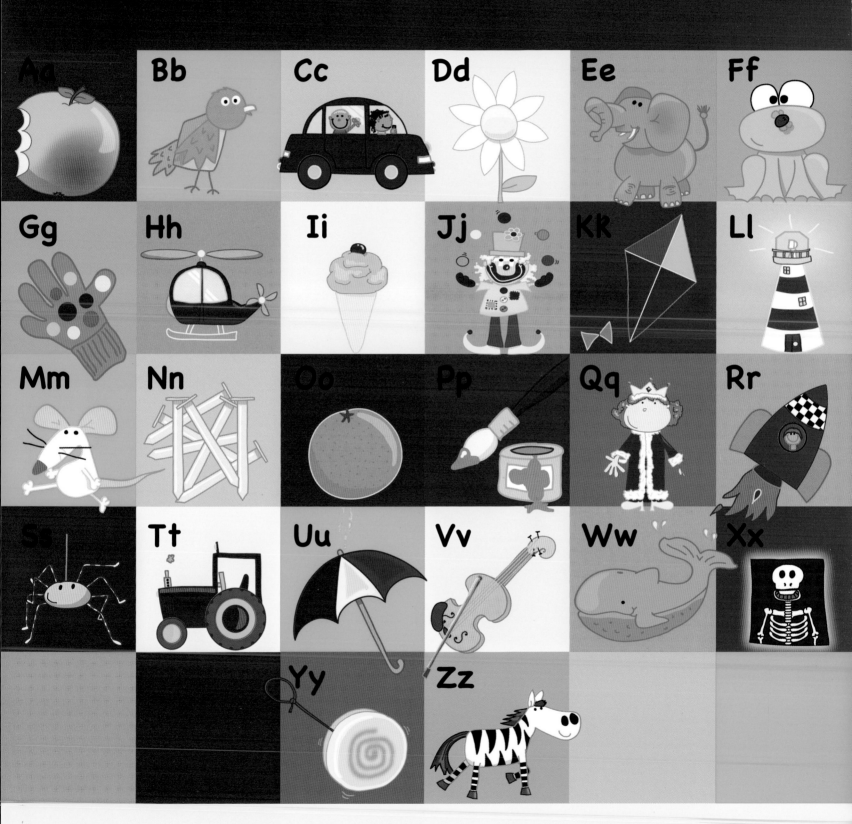

Aa Bb Cc Dd Ee Ff
Gg Hh Ii Jj Kk Ll
Mm Nn Oo Pp Qq Rr
Ss Tt Uu Vv Ww Xx
Yy Zz

igloobooks

Writing Letters

This book shows you how to write each letter of the alphabet.

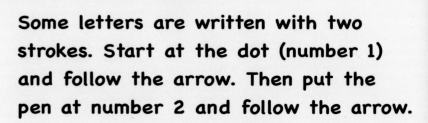

Some letters can be written with one stroke of the pen. Start at the dot (number 1) and follow the arrow to complete the letter.

Some letters are written with two strokes. Start at the dot (number 1) and follow the arrow. Then put the pen at number 2 and follow the arrow.

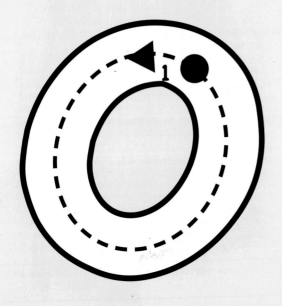

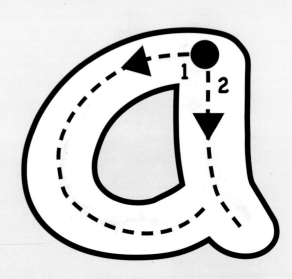

Children who hold a pen in their left hand write some letter strokes in a different direction to children who hold the pen in their right hand.

We write words from left to right.
Trace the line, starting at number 1.

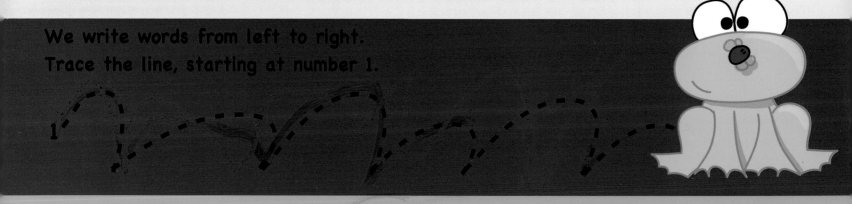

Start at number 1. Trace the bee's path.

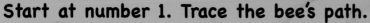

Letter shapes

Some letters are mostly round. These are based on circles.

a c e o

Trace the circles.

Some letters are based on straight lines.

i l j t f

Trace the straight lines.

Some letters use zigzags.

V v W w

Trace the zigzag lines.

Some letters use arches.

h n m u

Trace the arched lines.

Circle the letter a in the words below.

Aa

a is for...

arm

apron

apples

Trace the letter A.

acorn

Trace the zig-zag shape.

ant

Draw a line inside the letter shapes.

Trace the dotted lines.

Join the dots.

Try to write the letter yourself.

_____ _____

_____ _____

Circle the letter b in the words below.

Bb

b is for...

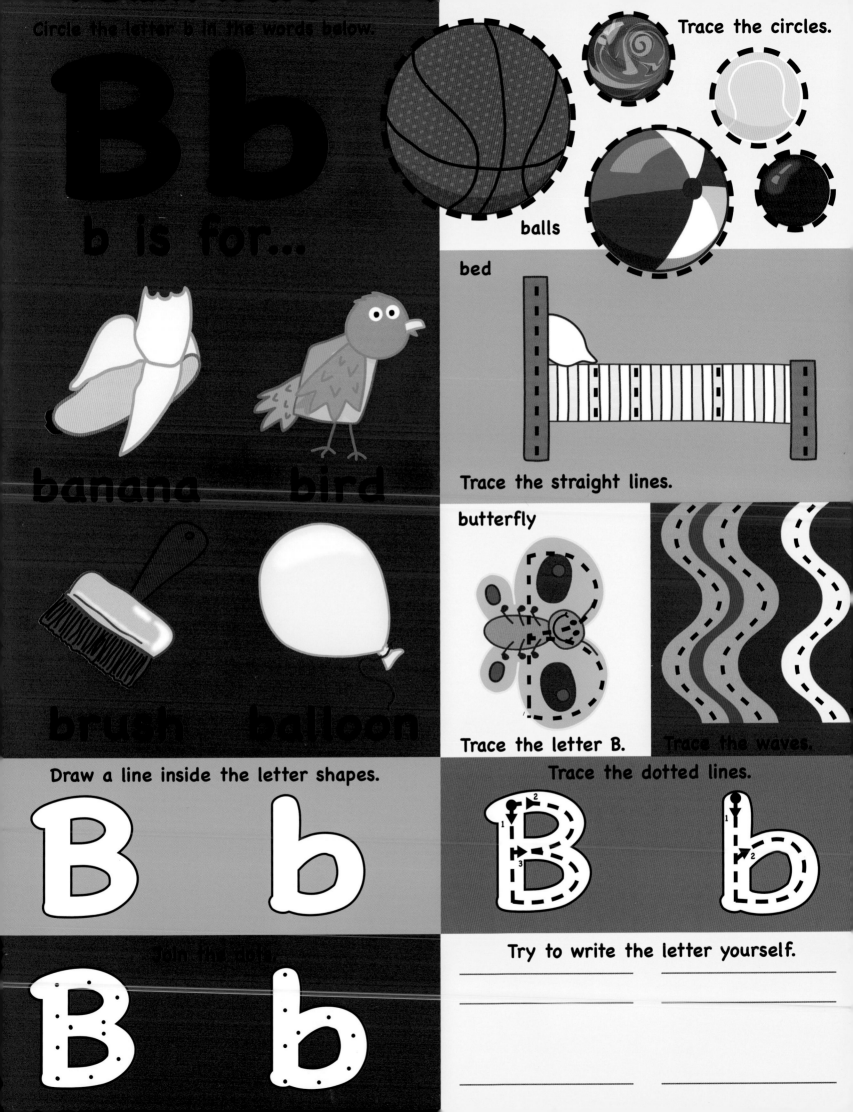

banana

bird

brush

balloon

Trace the circles.

balls

bed

Trace the straight lines.

butterfly

Trace the letter B.

Trace the waves.

Draw a line inside the letter shapes.

B b

Trace the dotted lines.

B b

Join the dots.

B b

Try to write the letter yourself.

_____ _____

_____ _____

Cc

Circle the letter c in the words below.

c is for...

clock

car

caterpillar

cow

carrot

Trace the c shapes.

Trace the letter C.

cup

Trace the c shapes.

cake

Draw a line inside the letter shapes.

Trace the dotted lines.

Join the dots.

Try to write the letter yourself.

Circle the letter d in the words below.

Dd

d is for...

dinosaur   doll

drum   dolphin

Trace the straight lines.

daisy

Trace the letter D.

dog

Trace the shapes.

dress

Draw a line inside the letter shapes.

Trace the dotted lines.

Join the dots.

Try to write the letter yourself.

_____   _____

_____   _____

_____   _____

Circle the letter e in the words below.

E e

e is for...

envelope   ear

engine

eye   elephant

Trace the smoke trail shape.

Trace the E shape.

Trace the dotted line.

Draw a line inside the letter shapes.

Join the dots.

Try to write the letter yourself.

Circle the letter f in the words below.

F f

f is for...

fish   firework

foot   frog

Circle the letter g in the word below.

G g

g is for... gorilla

Trace the circles.   Trace the shapes.

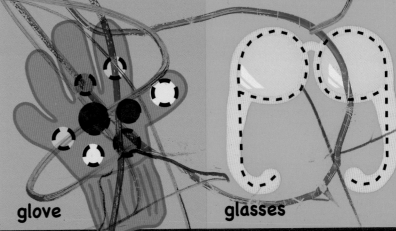

glove   glasses

Trace the dotted lines.

 F f

G g

Try to write the letter yourself.

Try to write the letter yourself.

Circle the letter h in the words below.

Hh

h is for...

hippo   hammer

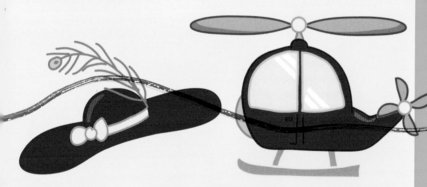

hat   helicopter

Trace the shapes.

house

Trace the letter H.

horse

Trace the shape.

heart

Draw a line inside the letter shapes.

H   h

Trace the dotted lines.

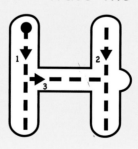

Join the dots.

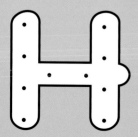

Try to write the letter yourself.

_____   _____

_____   _____

_____   _____

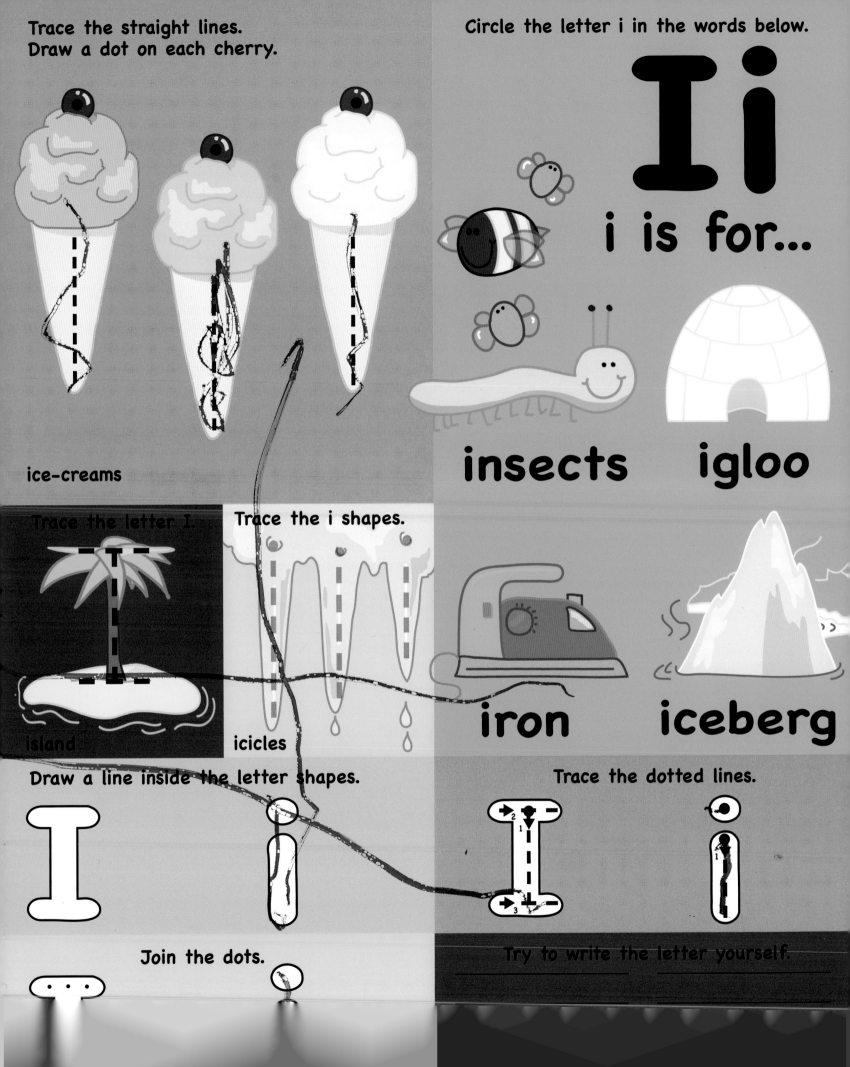

Trace the straight lines.
Draw a dot on each cherry.

Circle the letter i in the words below.

Ii

i is for...

ice-creams

insects   igloo

Trace the letter I.

Trace the i shapes.

island   icicles

iron   iceberg

Draw a line inside the letter shapes.

Trace the dotted lines.

Join the dots.

Try to write the letter yourself.

Complete the letter J in the words below.

Jj

j is for...

Jewels

jug

Trace the j shape.

Trace the j shape.

juggler

Trace the shapes.

Trace the j shapes.

jellyfish

Draw a line inside the letter shapes.

J j

Trace the dotted lines.

2 → 1 J 1 j

Join the dots.

J j

Try to write the letter yourself.

_____   _____

_____   _____

_____   _____

Trace the shapes.

kites

Circle the letter k in the words below.

K k

k is for...

key   kangaroo

koala   kitten

Trace the letter K.

kettle

Trace the shape.

king

Draw a line inside the letter shapes.

K k

Trace the letter K.

Join the dots.

K k

Try to write the letter yourself.

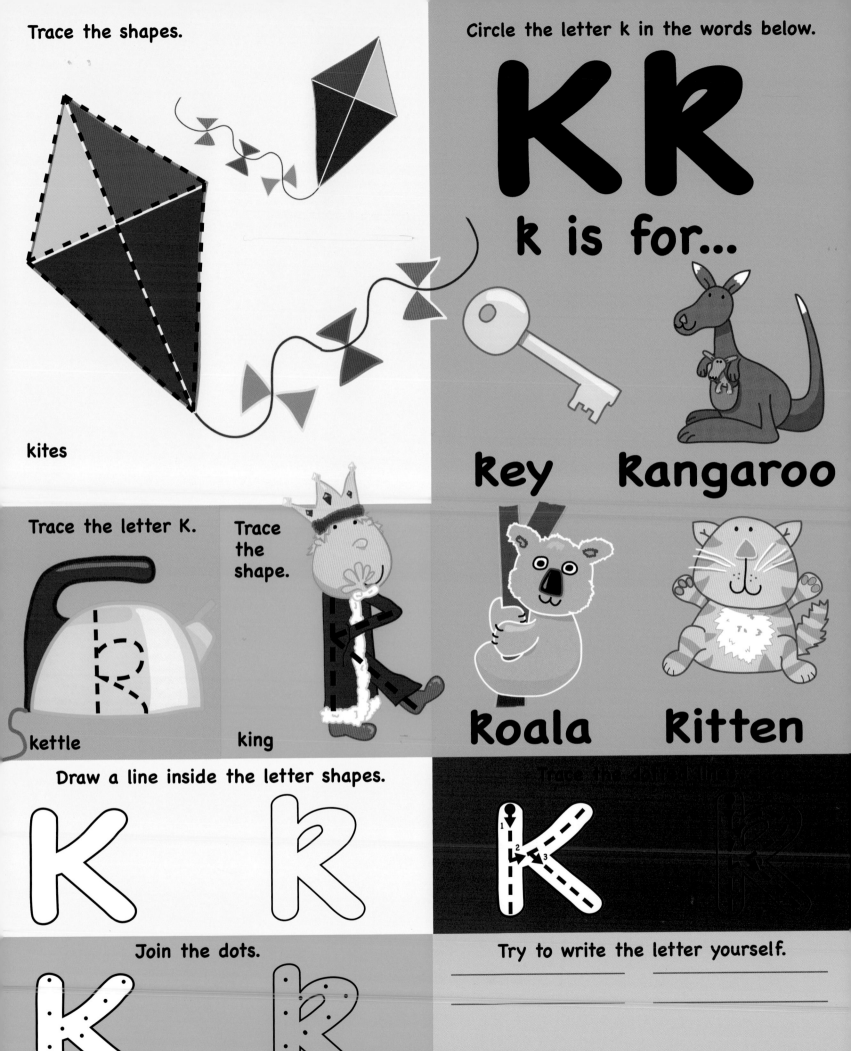

Circle the letter l in the words below.

Ll

l is for...

lion   lemon

leaf lighthouse

Trace the lines.

lines

ladder   legs

Trace the letter L.   Trace the l shapes.

Draw a line inside the letter shapes.

Trace the dotted lines.

Join the dots.

Try to write the letter yourself.

Circle the letter m in the words below.

Mm

m is for...

moon

monkey   mouse

Trace the dotted lines.

M   m

Try to write the letter yourself.

_____

_____

Circle the letter n in the word below.

Nn

n is for...

nest

Trace the letter N.

nails

Trace the shapes.

Trace the dotted lines.

N   n

Try to write the letter yourself.

_____

_____

Circle the letter o in the words below.

Oo

o is for...

ostrich   onion   orchestra

octopus

Trace the circles.

Trace the letter O.

orange

Trace the circles.

owl

Draw a line inside the letter shapes.

Trace the dotted lines.

Join the dots.

Try to write the letter yourself.

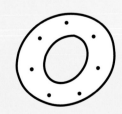

Trace the straight lines.

pencils

Trace the peas.

Trace the P shape.

paint

Trace the shapes.

pear

Draw a line inside the letter shapes.

Join the dots.

Circle the letter p in the words below.

Pp

p is for...

pig   penguin

pirate   piano

Trace the dotted lines.

Try to write the letter yourself.

_____   _____

_____   _____

Circle the letter q in the words below.

Qq

q is for...

queen

quilt

Trace the shape.

queen

Trace the shapes.

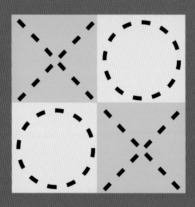

Trace the shapes.

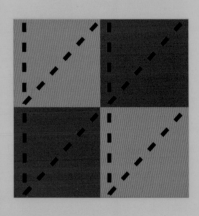

Draw a line inside the letter shapes.

Trace the dotted lines.

Join the dots.

Try to write the letter yourself.

Trace the shape.

road

Circle the letter r in the words below.

R r

r is for...

robot   rocket

rainbow   rake

Trace the letter R.

rope

Trace the shape.

rabbit

Draw a line inside the letter shapes.

R   r

Trace the dotted line.

R r

Join the dots.

R r

Try to write the letter yourself.

Circle the letter s in the words below.

Ss

s is for...

sandcastle **star**

spider

snowman

Trace the wavy lines.

Trace the wavy lines.

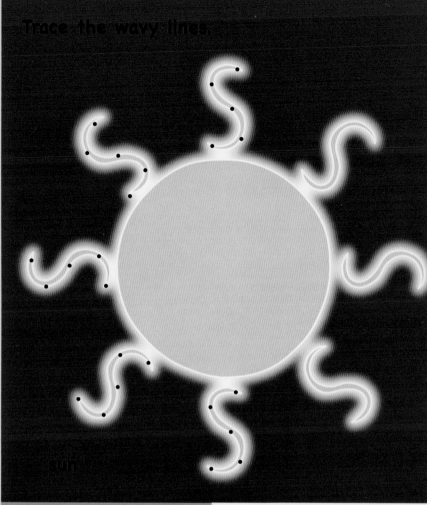

sun

Trace the S shape.

snake

Trace the s shape.

seahorse

Draw a line inside the letter shapes.

Trace the dotted lines.

Join the dots.

Try to write the letter yourself.

_____ _____

_____ _____

_____ _____

Circle the letter t in the words below.

Tt

t is for...

tiger   tractor

tree

toothbrush

Trace the dotted lines.

Try to write the letter yourself.

_____ _____

_____ _____

Circle the letter u in the word below.

Uu

u is for...

umbrella

Trace the shapes.

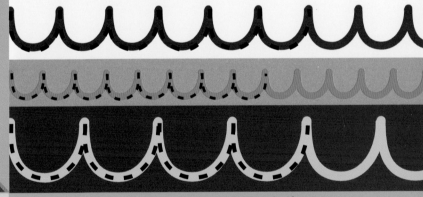

Trace the dotted lines.

Try to write the letter yourself.

_____ _____

_____ _____

Circle the letter V in the words below.

V V

v is for...

Trace the zigzag shape on the volcano.

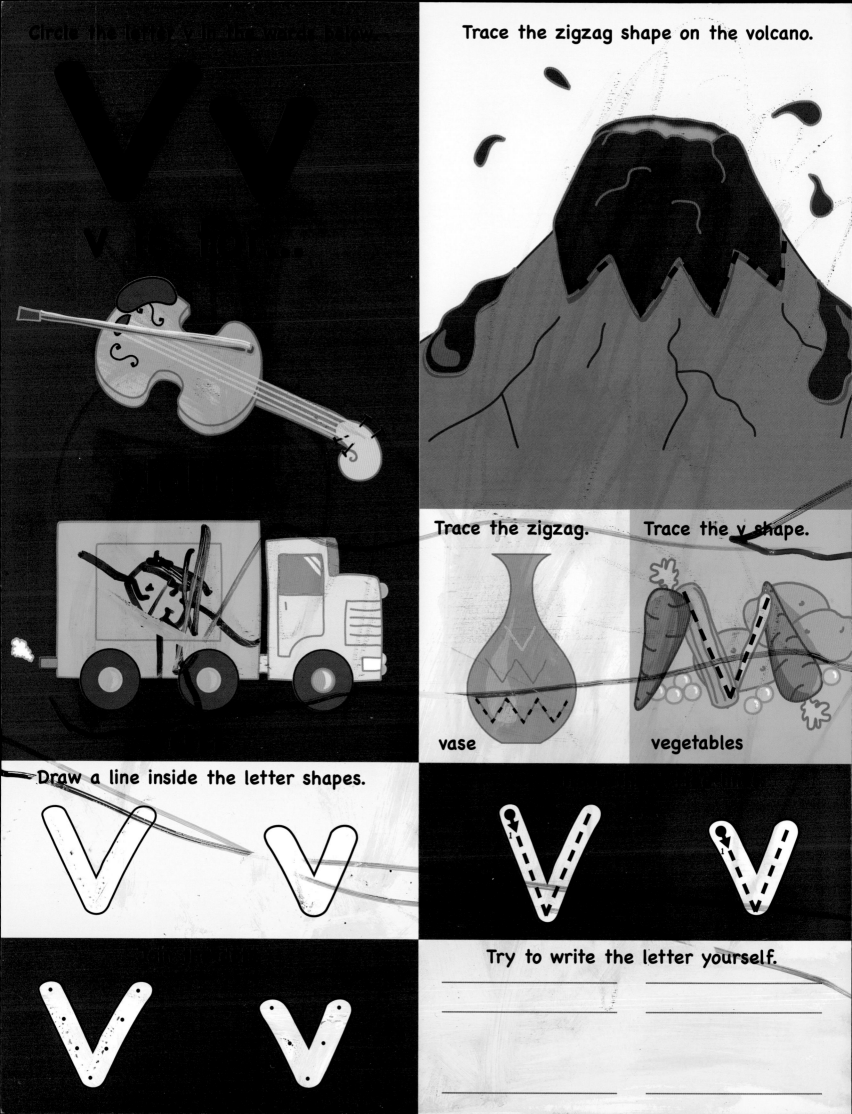

Trace the zigzag.

vase

Trace the v shape.

vegetables

Draw a line inside the letter shapes.

Try to write the letter yourself.

Trace the zigzag lines.

wall

Trace the zigzag.

web

Trace the zigzags.

waves

Circle the letter w in the words below.

Ww

w is for...

whale   window

watch   worm

Draw a line inside the letter shapes.

W

Trace the dotted lines.

W w

Join the dots

W W

Try to write the letter yourself.

Circle the x, y and z letters in the words below.

x is for...

x-ray

xylophone

y is for...

yo-yo

Trace the shape

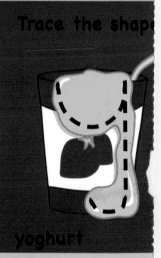

yoghurt

z is for...

zebra

Trace the shape

zigzags

Trace the dotted lines.

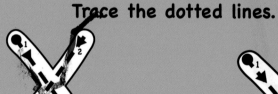

Trace the dotted lines.

Trace the dotted lines.

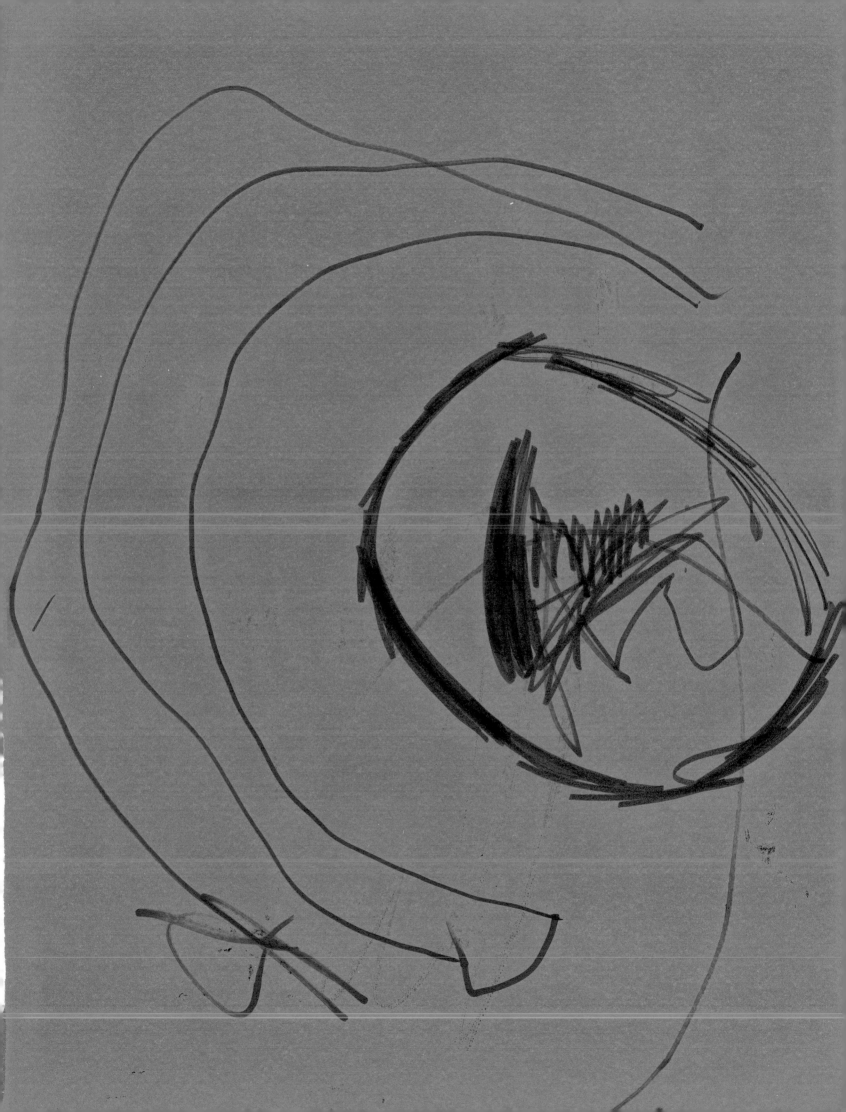